Lads & Da

Make Great 3D Decoupage Cards

Search Press

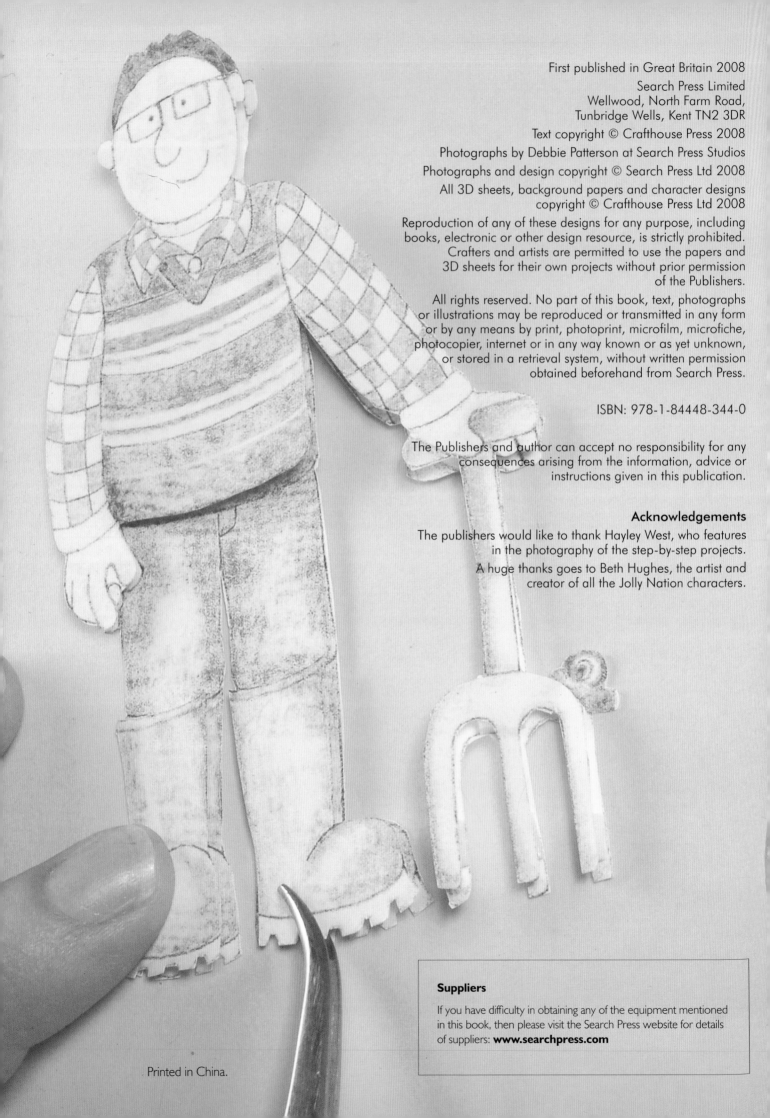

First published in Great Britain 2008
Search Press Limited
Wellwood, North Farm Road,
Tunbridge Wells, Kent TN2 3DR

ISBN: 978-1-84448-344-0

The Publishers and author can accept no responsibility for any
consequences arising from the information, advice or
instructions given in this publication.

Acknowledgements
The publishers would like to thank Hayley West, who features
in the photography of the step-by-step projects.
A huge thanks goes to Beth Hughes, the artist and
creator of all the Jolly Nation characters.

Suppliers
If you have difficulty in obtaining any of the equipment mentioned
in this book, then please visit the Search Press website for details
of suppliers: **www.searchpress.com**

Printed in China.

Contents

Introduction   4

    Materials   4

Football Boy   6

Gardening Man   10

Using the papers   16

Character papers   17

Background papers   32

Introduction

Since their launch back in January 2006 the Jolly Nation™ 3D decoupage characters have been used to create tens of thousands of fantastic and fun cards. There are now over eighty characters in the range and we are still adding more! Why are they so popular? Maybe it is because the characters remind us of real people we all know. Maybe it is because Jolly Nation™ decoupage is so easy to use, or maybe it is just that the characters look so cute when they are created, but one thing is for sure: Jolly Nation™ is here to stay!

Making cards for men or boys can sometimes be a tricky task. So many craft products are designed by women for women, that there is not always a huge choice of materials when it comes to making a card for your husband, son or grandson. But never fear, this book is packed with great male characters that are perfect for sending to the men in your life, so you never need to be short of inspiration again. We have made it nice and easy for you too, with step by step instructions and great project ideas. So what are you waiting for? Let's get crafting!

Materials

The following materials are needed to make the cards in this book, and they are all available from art and craft shops: card, card blanks, a craft knife and cutting mat, a pencil and ruler, large scissors, sharp scissors, 5mm (¼in) double-sided sticky foam squares, a pair of tweezers, an embossing stylus, a bone folder and photoglue.

From a golf-playing uncle, to a surfing son, there is a character to suit
just about everyone.

Football Boy

This smart and simple card is great for any football fan, and shows you how the three-dimensional decoupage builds up to make a really fantastic-looking piece.

It is also quick and easy to make and, more importantly, fun to give and receive!

1 Cut out the pieces of layers 1 and 2 from the Football Boy character paper.

2 Attach double-sided foam pads to the back of piece 2.

3 Remove the backing from the foam pads and place the piece on top of piece 1.

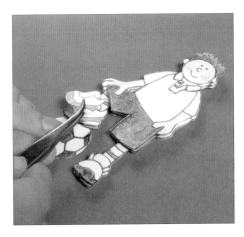

4 Cut out the body and shoes of layer 3. Attach foam pads to the backs of each piece, remove the backing, and secure in place on top of piece 2.

5 Repeat with the shirt and shoes of layer 4.

6 Add the collar and head of layer 5 in the same way.

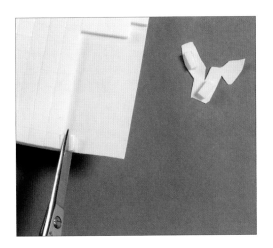

Tip

If you need to secure very small pieces, double-sided foam pads can be cut in half with sharp scissors.

7 Smear photoglue on to the back of the completed piece.

8 Place the piece in the centre of a card blank.

9 Cut out the small trophy and water bottle and attach them to the top right-hand corner with photoglue.

Opposite:

The finished card.

Often a simple design has the most impact. Less is more! Doubtless the boys you know have different interests, so pick a design that will speak to the recipient.

Gardening Man

Lots of men like to potter about in the garden, and this card is perfect for any green-fingered fellows in your life.

I Take a 31 x 15cm (12¼ x 6in) piece of card and use an embossing stylus and ruler to score vertical marks 10.3cm (4in) in from each side, as shown.

2 Measure 3cm (1¼in) up from the bottom edge of each side and make a mark with a pencil.

3 Draw a line from the top of each fold to the mark on the adjacent side.

4 Cut along each line to remove the corners of the card.

5 Fold the left side in, then fold it back on itself, using a bone folder to score the line.

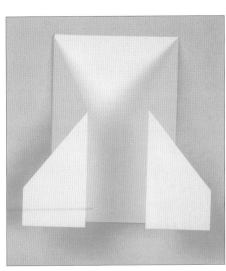

6 Repeat on the right-hand side to complete the basic card.

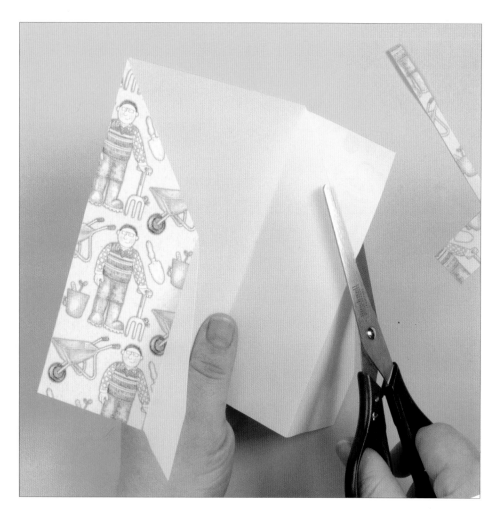

7 Cut two 5.5 x 17cm (2¼ x 6¾in) rectangles from the background paper, then stick them on to the folded card as shown with photoglue. Trim the excess along the corners.

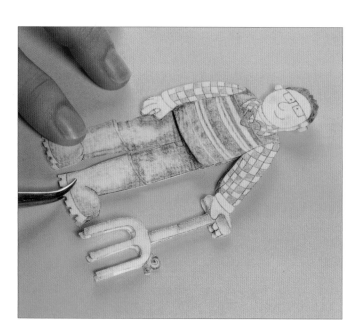

8 Cut out layers 1 and 2 of the figure from the Gardening Man paper. Attach double-sided foam pads to the back of the layer 2 pieces, remove the backing, and place them on top of the layer 1 piece.

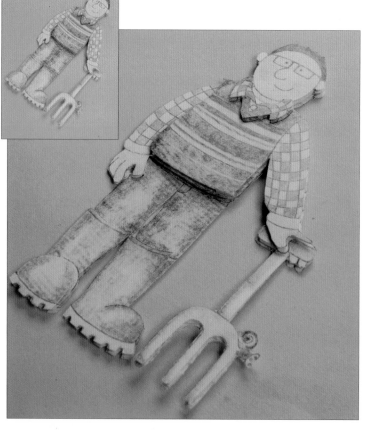

9 Repeat with layers 3 (see inset) and 4 to complete the gardening man.

10 Use photoglue to attach the man to the centre of the card, then cut out and attach the embellishments to the inside of the card as shown.

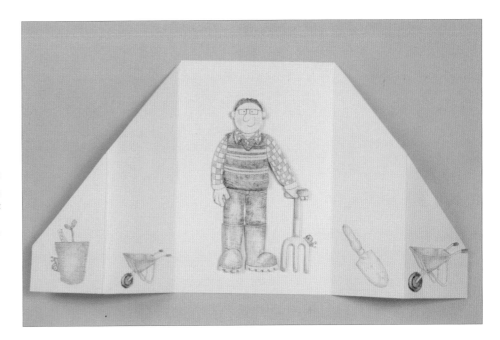

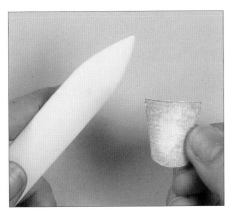

Tip
Use a bone folder to add a gentle curve to the flower pot.

11 Close the card and attach the wheelbarrow embellishment to the right-hand side using photoglue. Attach the flowerpot to the left-hand side using a foam pad.

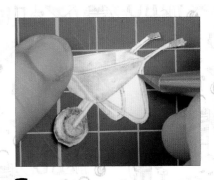

Tip
Use a craft knife and cutting mat to cut out small internal details, such as in the wheelbarrow.

Opposite:

The finished card.

Three-dimensional characters inside three-dimensional cards – guaranteed to stand out! Every man is different, so pick a picture that will make him chuckle.

Using the papers

Three-dimensional decoupage is the art of layering pieces of paper to give the impression of depth, and it works beautifully with these fun images to really give a bit of bounce to the finished cards. A flat picture is quickly transformed into a raised work of art, full of texture and interest – it is almost as though the character is jumping out at you!

The papers are grouped by character and background, so make sure you have the right pair once you have selected your subject.

Carefully fold and tear along the perforations near the spine of the book and remove the papers you intend to use. The numbers next to each image on the character paper show the order in which they should be mounted, starting from 1, as the bottommost layer, and counting upwards.

Good luck!

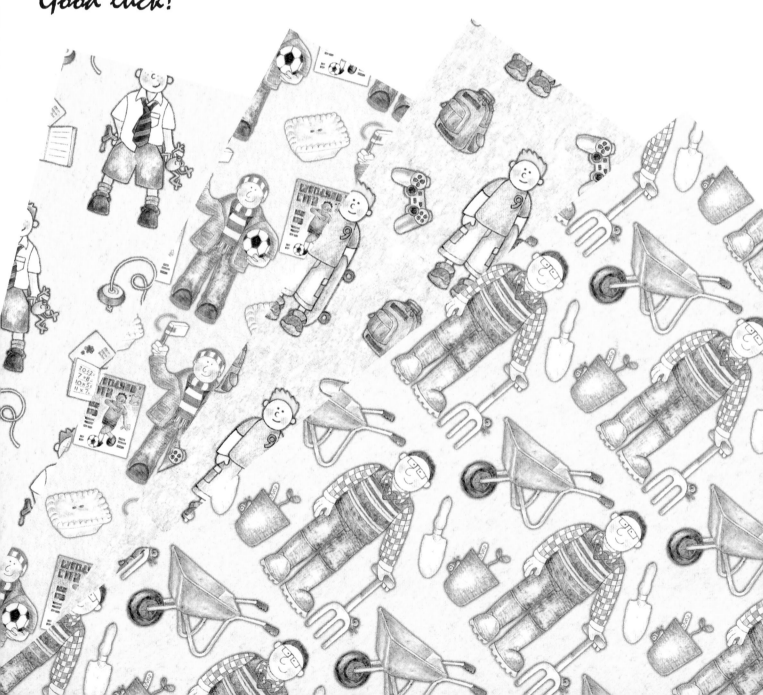

5

4

2

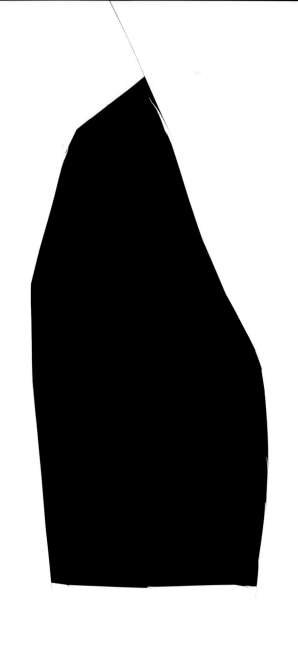

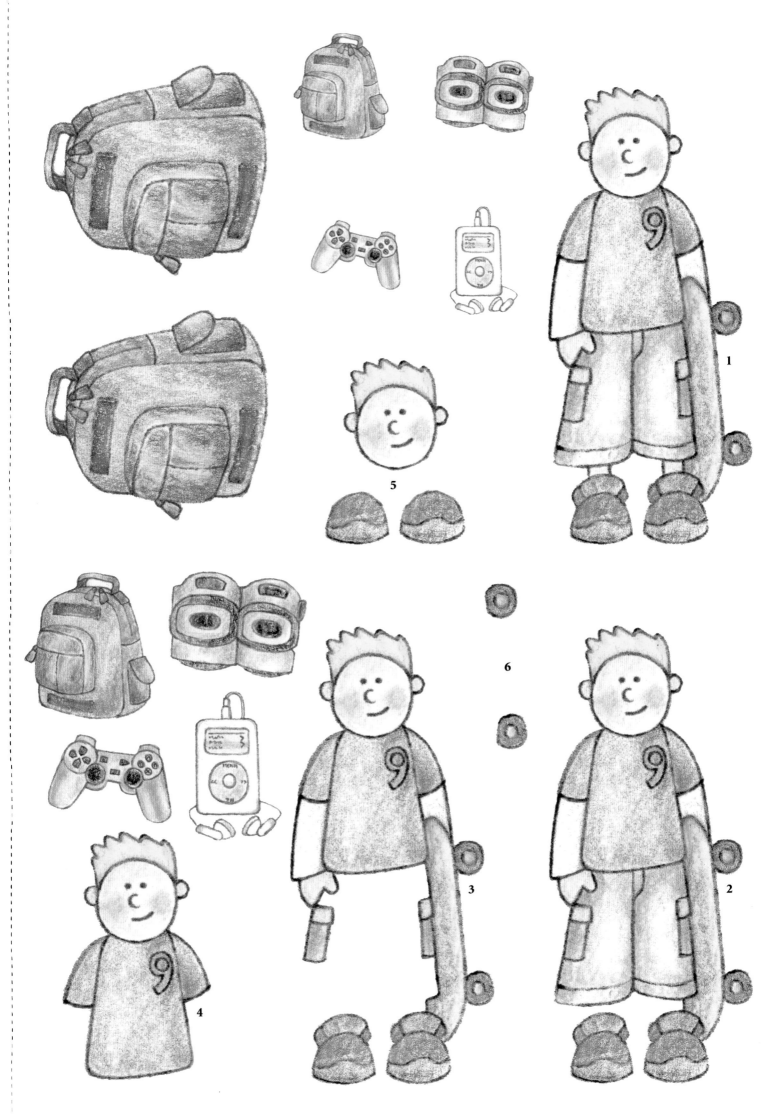

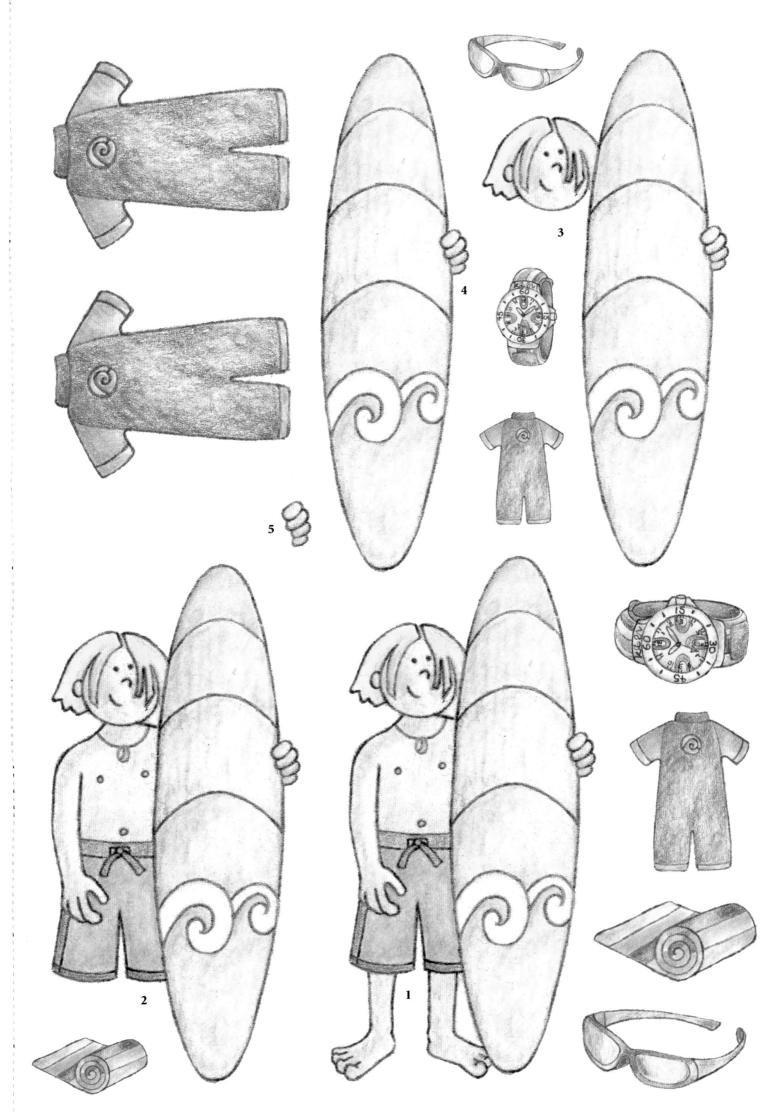

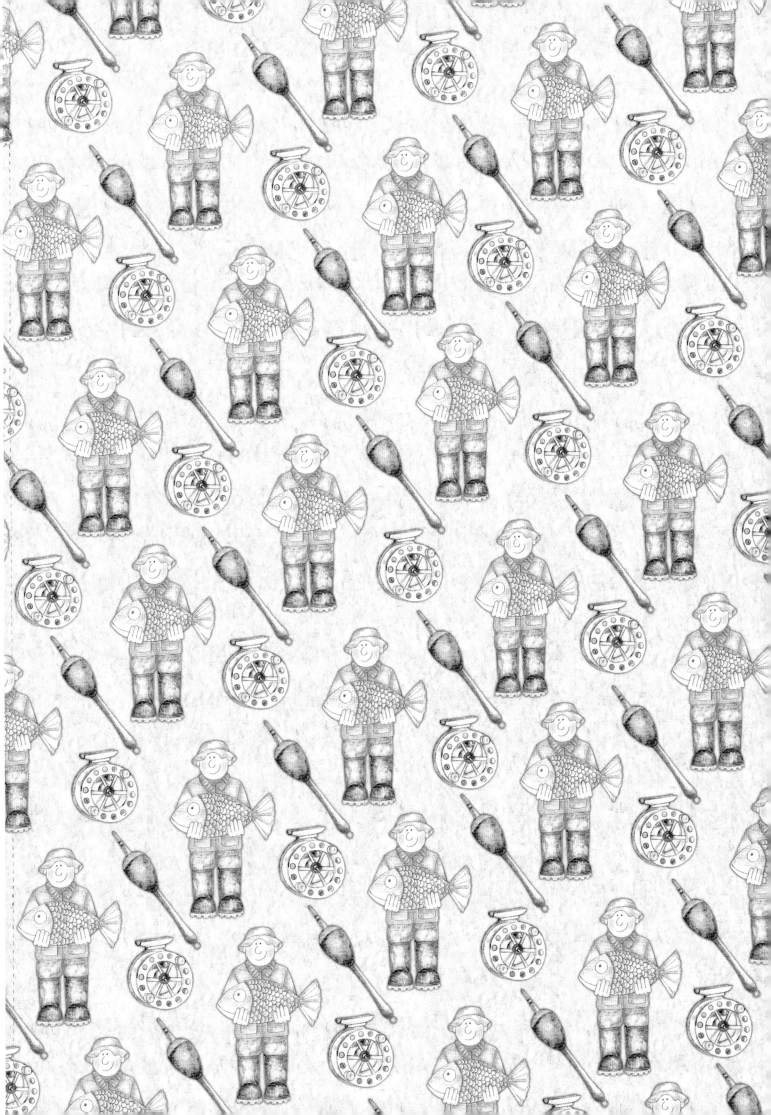

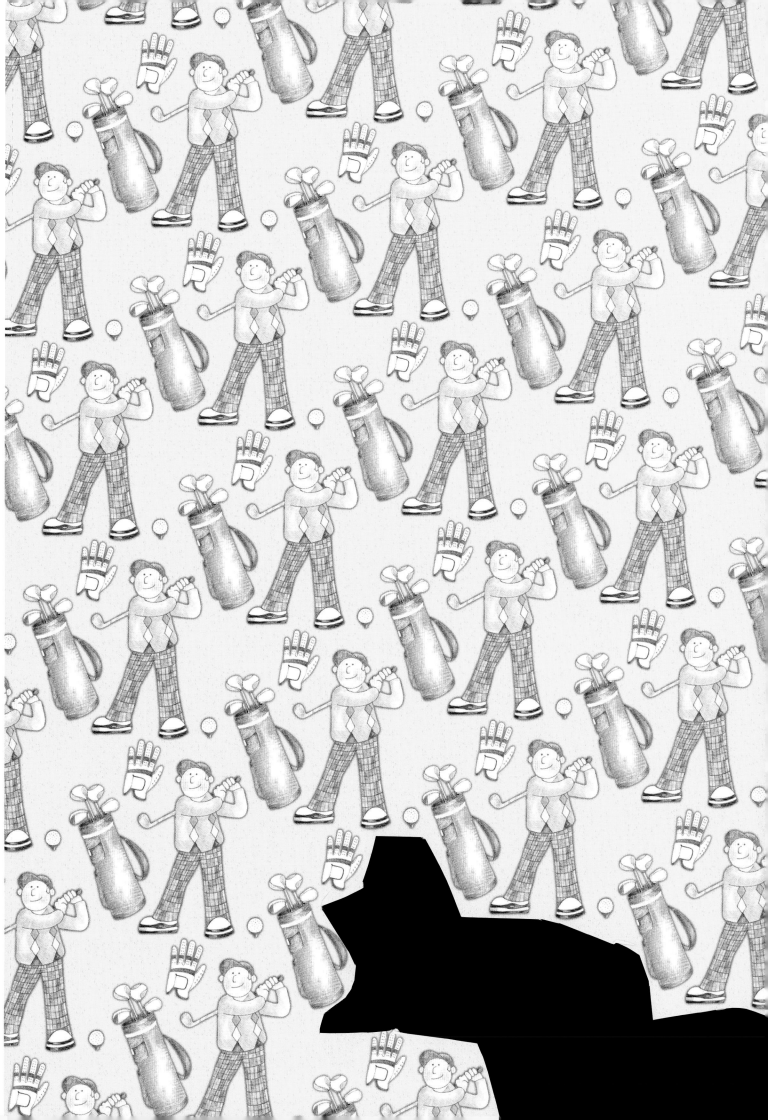